Liz Tames a Dragon (and her Anger) helps (their angry feelings and conflicts with others. Resear who develop self-control have better outcomes in adolescence and adulthood. **The Dunedin Multidisciplinary Health and Development Study** is an ongoing study conducted by the University of Otago in Dunedin, New Zealand. It is following a group of more than 1,000 people from birth to mid-life. The study identified self-control as observed throughout childhood as a significant predictor of health, wealth, and criminal activity in adulthood. According to researchers, early intervention makes a positive difference in adult behavior. When we help children verbalize and express emotions appropriately, we provide a lasting gift.

Praise for Liz Tames a Dragon:

"*Liz Tames A Dragon (and her Anger)* is a perfect tool for parents to use to empower their children to handle anger. Great illustrations and a kid-friendly story line make it super "user friendly" for even very young children -- and very frustrated parents. I highly recommend this book as a parent-driven way to help kids understand and manage their anger."

- *Susie Gregory, Parent Coach*

"My daughters play hard, love much, and argue OFTEN. They express frustrations and anger in different ways. This book gives great examples of dialogue and apologies and expressing feelings. We find ourselves now saying, 'Are you being a dragon right now?' because of this adorable and meaningful story."

- *Melissa Auvil, parent*

"*Liz Tames a Dragon* is a wonderfully engaging book that tells of an emotional journey of one young girl. The story is one that will touch the emotions and lives of children and parents alike. A children's book that is not only fun to read but also therapeutic in nature is a real treasure. Teaching our young children about the importance of emotional literacy, understanding emotions in themselves and others, and learning healthier ways to manage their emotions will increase the chances for successful outcomes in the future."

–*Susan Elswick EdD,LCSW,LSSW*

To Kara and Ella

– S.P.

Edited by **Jane Schneider**

Liz tames A Dragon (and her anger)

Written by
Stephanie Painter

Illustrated by
Jeanne Seagle

Liz simply loved Saturdays.

She chose a skating rink or park to visit, and her mom took her on special adventures.

Her baby sister often tagged along, but Liz didn't mind. While Meg napped, Liz ruled as

Queen of Saturday

Adventures.

But the more Meg grew, the less Liz was treated like a queen.

"Mom promised to take me to the movies on Saturday," Meg said.

"But I want to skate!" Liz replied in a huff.

you've Ruined my Saturday!

She stomped off to her room. There she found another awful surprise. Someone had drawn ugly crayon squiggles on her painting. Now Dad would never see the masterpiece she made for him.

"Meg, you colored on my painting, didn't you?" she shouted, her cheeks turning bright red. When Meg saw her sister's scary face, she trembled.

"I was just trying to make your picture prettier," she replied, her voice

sounding

small.

Liz felt hurt and sad, but mostly she felt MAD.

Just then, something strange began to happen. Green scales covered her legs, wings sprouted from her sides, and a dragon's heart thumped in her chest.

She shook her fists angrily.

at what you've done to me!

she **roared**.

"You make me scream and shout!"

Meg could turn her sister into a fire-breathing dragon.

"But how?" Liz wondered.

She had to find Meg's secret. So Liz charged into her sister's bedroom and dumped out all of the toys. She looked for a magic potion or ancient dragon spell.

Instead, she found only dirty socks and an old teddy bear.

"Tell me where you're hiding the magic potion!"
Liz hissed.

"I don't have any potion," Meg said as tears fell down her cheeks.

What? No potion, no spells? Liz was surprised.

She was sure that Meg had the power to change her into a powerful dragon. She peeked into the mirror. No dragon. Just a reflection of angry Liz, with a frightening scowl and red-hot cheeks. She looked again and then took a deep breath.

When she stopped yelling, her face felt cooler and her heart stopped pounding.

No one can make me act like a mean dragon, Liz thought.

Stomping around makes me feel strong, but my loud voice is scary.

Mom says it's okay to feel mad, but it's not okay to hurt my sister.

What if I find a not-so-scary way to let Meg know how I feel?

Liz put away the toys. Then she went to find her sister.

"I'm sorry I yelled at you," Liz said.

"I'm sorry I drew on your picture," said Meg.

Liz still felt a bit upset, so she took a long walk at the park to cool off.

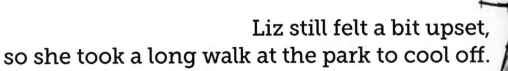

At bedtime, she promised herself,

"I will never act like a mean dragon again."

It turned out that taming a dragon was harder than she thought.

But Liz knew she could do it. The next day, Meg dragged Liz's favorite doll by the hair.

"Hey, that's my doll!" Liz cried. Her cheeks turned red, her body grew hot, and her mouth squished into a frown. But this time, she knew her body was trying to tell her,

"Stop. It's time to calm down."

She almost called her sister a dummy. Then she remembered how sad she felt when her best friend called her a name.

Instead, Liz could try something new.

She showed her sister how to carry the doll. "Would you carry Suzy this way?"

Meg understood calm words. She took the doll and held her carefully. Maybe Meg doesn't mean to be such trouble, thought Liz. But she still had to talk to Meg about the painting.

"I work hard on my paintings," Liz said. "I don't like it when you draw on them."

"I'd be mad, too, if you drew on my picture," Meg agreed.

Dragons breathe fire. Liz breathes kind, calm words. Dragons grow scales, and Liz grows more patience.

"You're Queen of Dragon Tamers," Meg said with a giggle.

"So how do you tame a dragon?" she asked.

Here's how you do it!

Liz knows that a smart kid can fix problems better than a mean, fire-breathing dragon. She tells herself, "No one can make me act like a dragon. I can control what I do and say."

Now when she feels mad, Liz takes big, deep breaths until her heart stops pounding. She waits to talk until she feels cool and calm.

She can draw and scribble out her angry feelings.

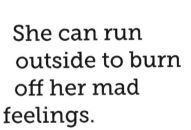

She can run outside to burn off her mad feelings.

She can pat her arms and give herself a nice butterfly hug.

Activity Guide

for Parents and Child Therapists

By Marlo Carney Zarzaur, ED.D., LPC-MHSP

Anger is a feeling that everyone has at one time or another. Anger is actually a healthy thing because it is your body's way of communicating with you and telling you that you do not like what is happening to you. Anger becomes a problem when it grows too big, too fast and takes over our thoughts, words, and actions.

One of the best things a parent can do for his or her child is to model appropriate expression of feeling. Parents can help their children identify their feelings and verbalize them appropriately.

Dragons Feel Sad, Too. Angry outbursts often start when a child feels embarrassed, disappointed, or sad. To help your child build a "feelings vocabulary," cut out pictures from magazines that show people who appear happy, sad, mad, excited, scared, and embarrassed. Paste the pictures on paper to make feelings cards. When your child is struggling, she can find a picture that shows her feeling and use words to describe the feeling.

What Makes My Dragon Grow? Help your child identify situations that trigger his anger. Hide eight to 10 items such as plastic dragons, jelly beans, or small toys. While your child hunts for the items, stop as each one is found and discuss something that fuels his anger. For example, he may feel angry when his sister takes toys without asking. Make a list of these anger triggers.

How Do I Know When My Dragon is Growing? Draw a dragon figure and ask your child, "How does your body feel when you are mad?" Headaches, increased heart rate, and sweaty palms are some physical symptoms of anger. Then ask your child to color 'hot spots' on the dragon's body.

Pay Attention! Your Dragon is Growing. Create a warning word or signal to share when you see your child struggling. Your child can also use the signal to help let others know when she is reaching her limit.

Cooling Down My Dragon. Teach your child techniques that will help him calm down. The techniques are physical, auditory, creative, and visual.

-Breathe in through your nose and hold your breath and count to three. Then breathe out while counting to three.

-Listen to calm music

-Draw or paint

-Use humor and make a silly face or enjoy a silly book

-Look at something that helps you feel calm. If it calms your child to watch fish swim in a fish tank, that would be a good choice for her.

Let the Dragon Out Safely. Make a dragon sock and fill it with modeling dough, squeeze balls, paper, maracas, bubble wrap, and popsicle sticks. Popping bubble wrap, breaking popsicle sticks, and tearing paper will help your child release tension.

Physical activity that increases the heart rate for 30 minutes a day helps our bodies let go of stress and anger in a healthy way. We feel happy after this kind of exercise and are more able to handle what comes our way. A child can burn off angry energy by jumping rope, running outside, or scribbling hard on paper.

Help your child express his feelings without blaming others. Encourage him to use 'I-statements.' For example, he could say, "I feel mad when my brother plays with my toy," not "My brother makes me mad."

Marlo Carney Zarzaur is a Licensed Professional Counselor who earned her Doctorate in Counseling at the University of Memphis. The focus of her practice is treating children, adolescents and young adults ages 3-25. Dr. Zarzaur is licensed and nationally certified as a mental health counselor, a school counselor, and an elementary school teacher.

Art Activities

How Do I Know When My Dragon Is Growing?

When Liz feels angry, her cheeks turn bright red and her heart beats faster. How does your body change when you feel angry?

Color 'hot spots' on the dragon's body

Cooling Down My Dragon

When Liz feels mad, she draws and scribbles out her angry feelings.
Do you like to draw or paint?

This page is for your pictures

Can you draw an angry dragon?

a calm dragon?

excited angry loving disappointed surprised

sad worried happy frustrated bored

confused calm embarrassed proud scared

My Many Feelings

Help your children understand their emotions by first giving the feelings names and then encouraging them to talk about how they are feeling. For example, you might say to your child, "Grandpa left on a trip, you are sad. You said you miss him."

Be sure to give children lots of opportunities to identify feelings in themselves and others. You might say, "Going to the park is so much fun. I see you smiling. Are you happy?" Or: "Kevin fell down and bumped his head. How do you think Kevin feels?"

Offer praise when your child begins to use words to describe feelings. When children choose words over fast reactions, they are on the way to developing more self-control, understanding of themselves, and quality relationships with others.

Made in the USA
San Bernardino, CA
11 July 2014